Reframing America was first published by the Center
for Creative Photography on the occasion of the
three-part series POINTS OF ENTRY created by the
Museum of Photographic Arts, San Diego; the
Center for Creative Photography, Tucson; and
The Friends of Photography, San Francisco.

Michael Read, POINTS OF ENTRY
   Publication Coordinator
Rupert Jenkins, POINTS OF ENTRY
   Production Editor
Designed by Toki Design, San Francisco

Library of Congress Catalog Card Number
95-076804

ISBN 0-8263-1769-3

Printed in Hong Kong by C & C Printing Co., Ltd.

Cover: **John Gutmann**, *"Yes, Columbus Did Discover America!"*
San Francisco, 1938. Gelatin silver print, 29.1 by 36.4 cm.
Center for Creative Photography

Preceding page: **Alexander Alland**, *A Gypsy Girl*, 1940. Gelatin
silver print, 23.7 by 16.4 cm. Courtesy Howard Greenberg
Gallery, New York

REFRAMING AMERICA

Alexander Alland

Otto Hagel & Hansel Mieth

John Gutmann

Lisette Model

Marion Palfi

Robert Frank

Essays by Andrei Codrescu and Terence Pitts

Center for Creative Photography   Tucson

University of New Mexico Press   Albuquerque

POINTS OF ENTRY has been made possible by a major grant from the Lila Wallace—Reader's Digest Fund

The entire POINTS OF ENTRY three-part exhibition series, catalogues, national tour, and educational programming has been made possible by a major grant from the

LILA WALLACE—READER'S DIGEST FUND

A Nation of Strangers
Reframing America
Tracing Cultures

Additional support for the national tour and promotion of POINTS OF ENTRY has been generously

provided by **✳ Metropolitan Life Foundation**

POINTS OF ENTRY National Tour

Museum of Photographic Arts
San Diego, California
September, 1995

Center for Creative Photography
Tucson, Arizona
September, 1995

The Friends of Photography/
Ansel Adams Center for Photography
San Francisco, California
September, 1995

International Museum of Photography
   at George Eastman House
Rochester, New York
April, 1996

National African American
   Museum Project
Smithsonian Institution
Washington, DC
August, 1996

High Museum of Art
Nexus Contemporary Art Center
Jimmy Carter Presidential
   Library-Museum
Atlanta, Georgia
February, 1997

Center for the Fine Arts
Miami, Florida
September, 1997

THIS CATALOGUE DOCUMENTS ONE OF THREE EXHIBITIONS that together constitute POINTS OF ENTRY, a unique collaboration among three photography museums intended to focus attention on one of the central defining issues of American life: immigration.

Photography can teach us a great deal about what immigration means within the context of American culture. For the past century and a half, photographers have documented the faces and experiences of those who immigrated to this country. Many of America's finest photographers have been immigrants themselves, and the work they produced in this country has expanded our artistic boundaries and deepened our understanding of the complexities and contradictions inherent to a nation of immigrants. And today, many younger artists are looking at the experience of immigration as a key to comprehending their own cultural heritages and identities.

As a series, POINTS OF ENTRY seeks to expand the discussion about the meanings and impact of immigration through photography. Some of those photographs are historical images found in archives across the country, some are among the classic works of art of the twentieth century, some have been created by a new generation of artists. Together they constitute a rich panorama of artistic responses to the subject of immigration and cultural differences.

To create such a complex and important project, three museums in three different communities joined together in a collaborative effort, supported by a major grant from the Lila Wallace–Reader's Digest Fund and with additional support from Metropolitan Life Foundation. The Museum of Photographic Arts (San Diego) initiated the collaboration and secured the project funding. The exhibitions, catalogues, and programming were created and produced in a partnership that involved the artistic and administrative staffs of the Museum of Photographic Arts, the Center for Creative Photography (Tucson), and The Friends of Photography (San Francisco).

We are profoundly grateful to the Lila Wallace–Reader's Digest Fund for its visionary grant, which enabled the consortium to take the risk to create POINTS OF ENTRY, and to Metropolitan Life Foundation, which stepped forward to support the national tour and its promotion at a crucial time in its development. Among the exceptional collaborators on the project have been Vicki Goldberg, guest curator for the Museum of Photographic Arts; Andrei Codrescu, Rebecca Solnit, and Ronald Takaki, guest essayists for the catalogues; and Catherine S. Herlihy, bibliographer. We thank them for their contributions, as we thank the literally hundreds of others across the country who provided support, guidance, advice, contacts, original art, and loans of historical materials.

The American public today is being exposed to a wide range of information and opinions about immigration and its impact on our culture. Many of the debates now taking place have roots that extend deep into American history. We hope that the efforts of the artists, scholars, writers, and researchers presented here will promote a fuller understanding of the richness of the American cultural experience, past, present, and future.

Terence Pitts, Director, Center for Creative Photography
Arthur Ollman, Director, Museum of Photographic Arts
Andy Grundberg, Director, The Friends of Photography

Contents

Whose woods these are I think I know.

His house is in the village though;

He will not see me stopping here

To watch his woods fill up with snow.

— Robert Frost
Stopping by Woods on a Snowy Evening

NOTES OF AN ALIEN SON

BY ANDREI CODRESCU

AFTER HAVING BEEN IN AMERICA for nearly thirty years, I am only an immigrant when people want me to talk about it. Paradoxically, it was a recent return to Romania, my native country, that caused me to re-evaluate my American experience. Until that time, I considered myself a model American: drank Jim Beam, wore Converse hightops, quit smoking on tax day. Of course, I may have been *too* perfect.

I went back to Romania in December 1989 to report on the so-called revolution over there, but in truth I went back in order to smell things. I went there to recover my childhood. I touched the stones of the medieval tower under the Liars' Bridge, where I used to lie still like a lizard in the summer. I put my cheek against the tall door of our old house, built in 1650, with its rusty smell of iron. I sniffed at people's windows to see what they were cooking. There were aromas of paprikash and strudel, and the eternal cabbage.

I made my way into the past through my nose, madeleinizing everything. My childhood, which had been kept locked and preserved in the crumbling city of Hermanstadt, was still there, untouched. It had outlasted my emigration. It was a thousand years old.

Considering, then, that childhood lasts for a thousand years, the past thirty years of adulthood in America do not seem like such a big deal. My old Romanian friends, now adults, had metamorphosed in those three decades into—mostly—fat survivors of a miserable and baroque system where material things were the supreme spiritual value. For them, America was the heavenly Wal-Mart. That's what God was during Communism, because God was everything, and everything can be found at Wal-Mart. Forty years of so-called Communism had done no more than polish to perfection my grandmother's maxim, "In America dogs walk around with pretzels on their tails." Loose translation: In America the sidewalks are paved with gold.

I used to fantasize coming back to my country a celebrated author,

Facing page: **Alexander Alland,** Untitled, 1948. Gelatin silver print, 26.6 by 34.1 cm. Center for Creative Photography

envied by all the people who made my life hell in high school. But now I wished, more than anything, that I'd come back as a Wal-Mart. If only I were a Wal-Mart, I could have spread my beauteous aisles to the awe-struck of Hermanstadt and fed them senseless with all the bounty of America.

When I returned to the United States, I reeled about for a few days in shock. Everything was so new, so carelessly abundant, so thoughtlessly shiny, so easily taken for granted. The little corner store with its wilted lettuce and spotted apples was a hundred times more substantial than the biggest bareshelf store in Romania.

My mother, ever a practical woman, started investing in furniture when she came to America. Not just any furniture. Sears furniture. Furniture that she kept the plastic on for fifteen years before she had to conclude, sadly, that Sears wasn't such a great investment. In Romania, she would have been the richest woman on the block.

Which brings us to at least one paradox of immigration. Most people come here because they are sick of being poor. They want to eat and they want to show something for their industry. But soon enough it becomes evident to them that these things aren't enough. They have eaten and they are full, but they have eaten alone and there was no one with whom to make toasts and sing songs. They have new furniture with plastic on it but the neighbors aren't coming over to ooh and aah. If American neighbors or less recent immigrants do come over, they smile condescendingly at the poor taste and the pathetic greed. And so, the greenhorns find themselves poor once more: This time they are lacking something more elusive than salami and furniture. They are bereft of a social and cultural milieu.

My mother, who was middle class by Romanian standards, found herself immensely impoverished after her first flush of material well-being. It wasn't just the disappearance of her milieu—that was obvious—but the feeling that she had, somehow, been had. The American supermarket tomatoes didn't taste at all like the rare genuine item back in Romania. American chicken was tasteless. Mass-produced furniture was built to fall apart. Her car, the crowning glory of her achievements in the eyes of folks back home, was only three years old and was already beginning to wheeze and groan. It began to dawn on my mother that she had perhaps made a bad deal: She had traded in her friends and relatives for ersatz tomatoes, fake chicken, phony furniture.

Leaving behind your kin, your friends, your language, your smells, your childhood, is traumatic. It is a kind of death. You're dead for the home folk and they are dead to you. When you first arrive on these shores you are in mourning. The only consolation are these products, which had been imbued with religious significance back at home. But when these things turn out not to be the real things, you begin to experience a second death, brought about by betrayal. You begin to suspect that the religious significance you had attached to them was only possible back home, where these things did not exist. Here, where they are plentiful, they have no significance whatsoever. They are inanimate fetishes, somebody else's fetishes, no help to you at all. When this realization dawned on my mother, she began to rage against her new country. She deplored its rudeness, its insensitivity, its outright meanness, its indifference, the chase after the almighty buck, the social isolation of most Americans, their inability to partake in warm, genuine fellowship and, above all, their deplorable lack of awe before what they had made.

This was the second stage of grief for her old self. The first, leaving her country, was sharp and immediate, almost tonic in its violence. The second was more prolonged, more damaging, because no hope was attached to it. Certainly not the hope of return.

And here, thinking of return, she began to reflect that perhaps there had been more to this deal than she'd first thought. True, she had left behind a lot that was good, but she had also left behind a vast range of daily humiliations. If she was ordered to move out of town she had to comply. If a party member took a dislike to her she had to go to extraordinary lengths to placate him because she was considered petit-bourgeois and could easily have lost her small photo shop. She lived in fear of being denounced for something she had said. And worst of all, she was a Jew, which meant that she was structurally incapable of obtaining any justice in her native land. She had lived by the grace of an immensely complicated web of human relations, kept in place by a thousand small concessions, betrayals, indignities, bribes, little and big lies.

At this point, the ersatz tomatoes and the faux chicken did not appear all that important. An imponderable had made its appearance, a bracing, heady feeling of liberty. If she took that ersatz tomato and flung it at the head of the Agriculture Secretary of the United States, she would be making a statement about the disastrous effects of pesticides and mechanized farming. Flinging that faux chicken at Barbara Mandrell would be equally dramatic and perhaps even media-worthy. And she'd probably serve only a suspended sentence. What's more, she didn't have to eat those things, because she could buy organic tomatoes and free-range chicken. Of course, it would cost more, but that was one of the paradoxes of America: To eat as well as people in a Third World country eat (when they eat) costs more.

My mother was beginning to learn two things: one, that she had gotten a good deal after all, because in addition to food and furniture they had thrown in freedom; and two, America is a place of paradoxes—one proceeds from paradox to paradox like a chicken from the pot into the fire.

And that's where I come in. My experience was not at all like that of my mother. I came here for freedom, not for food. I came here in the mid-sixties. Young people East and West at that time had a lot more in common with each other than with the older generations. The triple-chinned hogs of the *nomenklatura* who stared down from the walls of Bucharest were equal in our minds to the Dow Chemical pigs who gave us napalm and Vietnam. By the time I left Romania in 1966, the Iron Curtain was gone: A Hair Curtain fell between generations. Prague 1968 and Chicago 1968 were on the same axis. The end of the old world had begun.

Our anthems were the songs of Dylan, the Beatles, the Rolling Stones, all of whom were roundly despised by my mother because she was sure that such tastes would lead to our being thrown out of America. And she wasn't all that wrong: Her

BY THE TIME I LEFT ROMANIA IN 1966, THE IRON CURTAIN WAS GONE: A HAIR CURTAIN FELL BETWEEN GENERATIONS. PRAGUE 1968 AND CHICAGO 1968 WERE ON THE SAME AXIS. THE END OF THE OLD WORLD HAD BEGUN.

old don't-rock-the-boat instinct was an uncannily fine instrument. At that time, being anti-establishment in America could be perilous. But this wasn't Romania. The difference, the massive difference, was the constitutional right to freedom of speech and assembly. True, for a moment or two—and for several long, scary moments since—those constitutional rights were in real danger. And if Americans felt threatened, you can be sure that many niceties of the law simply didn't apply to refugees.

Nonetheless, I was drunk with freedom and I wasn't about to temper my euphoria with the age-old wariness of European Jews. My mother's main pleasure and strategy in those days was to overstuff me whenever

I came to visit. She believed that food would keep me safe. Food keeps you from going out at night, it makes you sleepy, makes you think twice about hitch-hiking, makes you, generally, less radical. The very things that alienated my mother—the speed, confusion, social unrest, absence of ceremony—exhilarated me. I had

IF SOMEBODY HAD ASKED ME, I WOULD HAVE SAID, "I'M A PLANETARY REFUGEE, A PROFESSIONAL REFUGEE, A PERMANENT EXILE." NOT ON MY CITIZENSHIP APPLICATION FORM, OF COURSE.

arrived here at an ecstatic moment in history and I was determined to make the most of it. And when, thanks to the marketing know-how of the CIA, I got to try LSD for the first time, I became convinced that freedom was infinitely vaster than was generally acknowledged. It was not just a right, it was an atmosphere. It was the air one needed to breathe. And one had to stay skinny.

In 1966, my generation welcomed me into its alienated and skinny arms with a generosity born of outsiderness. Young people at that time had become outsiders to America's mainstream. Those who went to Vietnam were way outside, even though, ostensibly, they served the inside. The others were in voluntary exile from the suburbs that immigrants hoped to live in one day. But what mattered is that we were all on the move. I happened to be a literal exile in a world of, mostly, metaphorical exiles. It was a match made in heaven. America was nineteen years old and so was I. I lived in a country of

exiles, a place that had its own pantheon of elders, exiled geniuses like Einstein and Nabokov, and whole nomad youth armies. Exile was a *place* in the mid-sixties, an international Idea-State, the only anarchist state in working order. It's not the kind of thing that comes around all that often in American immigrant history.

In the four hundred years since Europeans first came here, there have been many immigrant visions of America, most of them a variation of *Ubi pretzel ibi patria;* the true, ineffable one was not a pretzel but a pear—Charles Fourier's pear, to be exact. For Fourier, the pear was the perfect fruit. It was to be eaten in Paradise by lovers. This vision of a utopian New World was entirely about freedom. The freedoms granted by the Bill of Rights were only the steps leading to this new state of being.

The prophetic tradition maintains that America is chosen among nations to bring about the end of history. American utopian communities, which flourished here in the nineteenth century, were reborn with a vengeance a hundred years later. The possibility of utopia is an ingrained American belief, one that, it can be argued, has kept America strong, vigorous, and young. Walt Whitman's America was done with the niceties of Europe because it was bigger, ruder, and had a greater destiny. This America was also a country of immigrants who gave it their raw muscle and imagination. Diversity and industry were its mainstays.

Even Allen Ginsberg, a bitter prophet at the end of the 1950s, could say, "America, I put my queer shoulder to the wheel." Despite the irony, Ginsberg, the son of a Russian Jewish immigrant, really believes that his queer shoulder is needed, that America needs not just its bankers but also its queers.

But this sustaining vision of America is, paradoxically again, marginal. It is often confused with another, similar-sounding creed, which is in all the textbooks and is invoked by politicians on the Fourth of July. Immigrants are used as a rhetorical device to support the goals of the nation-state: America right or wrong. This is the official ideology, which, like the party line in Romania, is meant to drive underground the true and dangerous vision. Its faithful will admit to no contradiction between their love of freedom and their hatred of outsiders.

The history of public opinion on immigration shows mainly opposition to it. As the revolutionary ideas of the eighteenth century receded, compassion for the wretched and persecuted of the earth was dictated mainly by the interests of capitalists. Not that this was necessarily bad. Heartless capitalism in its ever-growing demand for cheap labor saved millions of people from the no-exit countries of the world. It was a deal that ended up yielding unexpected benefits: vigor, energy, imagination, the remaking of cities, new culture. Restless capital, restless people, ever-expanding boundaries—the freedom to move, pick up, start again, shed the accursed identities of static native lands. The deal turned out to have the hidden benefit of liberty. The liberty my mother discovered in America was here: It was a byproduct of the anarchic flow of capital, the vastness of the American space, *and* a struggle in the name of the original utopian vision. Of course, capitalism annexed the resulting moral capital and put on an idealistic face that it never started out with, and that it quickly sheds whenever production is interrupted. Nonetheless, it is this capitalism with a human face that brought most of us here.

But capitalism with a human face is not the same as the original vision of America. The original American dream is religious, socialist, and anti-capitalist. It was this utopianism—liberty in its pure, unalloyed state—that I experienced in non-denominational, ahistorical, uneconomical, transcendent flashes in the mid-sixties. It's not simple dialectical Manicheism we are talking about here. It's the mystery itself.

If somebody had asked my mother in the mid-sixties if she was a political refugee, she would have said, "Of course." But privately she would have scoffed at the idea. She was an economic refugee, a warrior in quest of Wal-Mart. In Romania she had been trained at battling lines for every necessity. In America, at last, her skills would come in handy. Alas. But if somebody had asked me, I would have said, "I'm a planetary refugee, a professional refugee, a permanent exile." Not on my citizenship application form, of course. That may have been a bit dramatic, but in truth I never felt like a refugee, either political or economic. What I felt was that it was incumbent upon me to manufacture difference, to make myself as distinct and unassimilable as possible. To increase my foreignness, if you will. That was my contribution to America: not the desire to melt in but the desire to embody an instructive difference.

To the question, "Whose woods are these?"—which Robert Frost never asked because he thought he knew the answer—my mother would have said, without hesitation, "Somebody else's." My mother, like most immigrants, knew only too well that these were somebody else's woods. She only hoped that one day she might have a piece of them. My answer to that question would have been, and I think it still is, "Nobody's." These are nobody's woods and that's how they must be kept: open for everybody, owned by nobody. This is, in part at least, how Native Americans thought of them. It was a mistake, of course. Nobody's woods belong to the first marauding party who claims them. A better answer might be: "These woods belong to mystery; this is the forest of paradoxes; *un bosche oscuro;* we belong to them, not they to us." ◄

by Terence Pitts

As the United States went through a series of drastic and sudden economic, social, and political evolutions between the early thirties and the end of the fifties, it is not surprising that American photography should also change dramatically. Looking back, it is easy to point to several catalysts for change. The Great Depression brought about the creation of federal agencies, such as the Farm Security Administration and the Works Progress Administration, with mandates to photographically document and articulate the times and to focus, for the first time ever, the attention of government-sponsored photographers on the social consequences of the nation's economic ills. At the same time, America's economy of mass consumption led to the development of mass-market magazines such as *Life* that incorporated photography for much of their substance. Then, too, the changing technology of photography itself, most notably the introduction of German-made, hand-held 35mm cameras in the mid-thirties, helped spawn a more casual, spontaneous, and unobtrusive form of image making. Finally, the creativity and commitment of photographers pushed the medium to new realms of expression in keeping with the changing times as they used photography to probe the invisible aspects of American society.

Many of the men and women who altered the course of American photography during these decades were European photographers who came to this country, fleeing revolution, fascism, war, and persecution and seeking the greater employment and artistic opportunities that this country was beginning to offer. Cumulatively, these emigrés brought with them many different artistic traditions and many different perspectives on issues such as class, politics, American-style capitalism, and race, allowing them to create an extraordinary aesthetic and documentary legacy that has influenced every succeeding generation of American photographers.

Throughout the entire history of photography in this country—beginning with the introduction of the French photographic process known as the daguerreotype toward the end of 1839—foreign-born men and women have taken up cameras and

Facing page: **Otto Hagel,** *The Window Washer,* 1939. Gelatin silver print, 34.1 by 26.4 cm. Center for Creative Photography.

made photographs for commercial and artistic consumption. They opened photographic portrait studios, photographed for business and the government, joined a myriad of amateur photographic societies and camera clubs, worked as photojournalists, and entered the ranks of the American art scene. Even a cursory glance through a standard history of the medium summons forth dozens of names of foreign-born photographers who practiced in this country: Alexander Gardner, Eadweard Muybridge, John K. Hillers, Jacob Riis, Arnold Genthe, Frank Eugene, Edward Steichen, Weegee, László Moholy-Nagy, Sonya Noskowiak, Martin Munkasci, Alfred Eisenstadt, Philippe Halsman, Ben Shahn, Jack Delano, Ernst Haas, Cornell Capa, Robert Capa, Gjon Mili, David "Chim" Seymour, Ruth Bernhard, Frederick Sommer, Eva Rubenstein, and Lucas Samaras, to select just a few.

At every stage of American photography, immigrant practitioners have been at the forefront. Arguably, though, Jacob Riis was the first to make his mark on American photography in a way that reflected his experience as an immigrant. In 1870 the twenty-one-year-old Riis emigrated from Denmark, ultimately finding a career as a reporter covering some of the poorest, most violent neighborhoods in New York City. Riis purchased a camera and a magnesium flash device, determined to visually depict the squalor and hopelessness of the city's slums. His seminal book *How the Other Half Lives*, published in 1890, used the newly invented halftone printing process to reproduce photographs that stood as an indictment of the American city and reframed the immigrant experience for all to see. Riis's untutored eye and basic innocence about the process of photography combined with his sheer determination resulted in pictures that conveyed essential truths in an appalling and unrelenting manner. Ansel Adams described looking at Riis's images as one of his few "intense experiences" in photography; and indeed, Riis's photography conveys an unyielding sense of integrity, technical simplicity, and startling clarity.

The purpose of *Reframing America* is not to celebrate the achievements of the many American photographers who happen to have been born abroad, nor is it to claim that they were alone in changing the aesthetic and social framework of their medium. Rather, *Reframing America* explores a quarter-century of American history when European emigrés were at the forefront of transforming photography in this country and creating a startling new vision of America. Included is the work of seven such photographers: Alexander Alland, Robert Frank, John Gutmann, Otto Hagel, Hansel Mieth, Lisette Model, and Marion Palfi. They arrived in this country between 1923 and 1947, seven among many photographers who landed here during those years. By themselves, these seven did not reformulate American photography, and to that extent, I submit them as representatives of a much larger group who share in the credit for the remarkable creativity in photography during this era. For the most part, these seven men and women were working photographers or artists before arriving in America. As such, they brought European artistic traditions and training with them. Their work pushed the photographic image to new emotional and psychological depths, bringing more and more of the artist's subjective response into what had largely been seen as an objective, image-making process.

Throughout the years between the two world wars, European photography was receptive to the avant-garde art movements that originated there: constructivism, dadaism, cubism, and surrealism. Unlike the situation in America, European modernist photography adventurously freed the medium from its own constricting self-definition. Nearly a century's worth of dos and don'ts were summarily overturned as many European photographers and artists accepted new approaches to photography: odd vantage points, photomontage, negative prints, collaging with other media, and the photographing of completely staged realities. Twentieth-century European visual experimentation encouraged artists to use photography as just another medium of plastic expression and encouraged photographers to exploit what American classical photographers perceived to be flaws in the medium: reflections, visual distortions due to movement or camera angle, visual elements that were out of focus, severe cropping of the visual field, and so on. Even the nature of the photographic print was viewed differently by European photographers. Many had worked commercially in studios or for publications, and most did not share in the near-obsession among American art photographers for the craft of making a photographic print; for the Americans, artistic vision and craftsmanship were inextricably linked.

In social terms, European emigré photographers often depicted, with remarkable power and insight, an America that was more complex and diverse and more deeply troubled than photography had revealed before. Partly because they looked at America with fresh eyes and partly because the America they found did not correspond to the America they expected, their work often directly addressed the issues that haunt this country: poverty, injustice, and intolerance. European photographers often probed the cultures that seemed to be "invisible in America," to quote the title of a book of Marion Palfi's photographs of African Americans, American Indians, Hispanic Americans, prisoners, the urban poor, and the elderly. From Alexander Alland's extended study of multicultural New York in the thirties to Robert Frank's raw and poetic images that depict, among other things, the stark racial separation in the fifties, race is a central theme in the body of European-emigré photography. At the same time, these artists responded photographically to daily life in their newly adopted homeland and in doing so identified quintessential American themes, such as the emerging cult of the automobile, Hollywood's glamorous but fictional America, jazz, and the blaring commercialism of American consumer culture.

Robert Frank's *The Americans*, which was published in the United States at the end of 1959, can be seen as a continuation of some of the same impulses that began seventy years earlier with Jacob Riis's *How the Other Half Lives.* Taken collectively, the work of the seven photographers in *Reframing America* provides a powerful, holistic vision of two turbulent, transitional decades in American history and in American photography. The America that they saw didn't always look like the America that those born and raised here saw. And the approach to photography that they used didn't always follow the prevailing conventions of mainstream American photography of the time. But out of these differences arose a new way of envisioning this country, of framing its complex social fabric within the small confines of a camera lens, and of making pictures that could have a profound effect in both social and artistic terms. ◄

ALEXANDER ALLAND

"I WAS BORN IN SEVASTOPOL, a city in Southern Russia, and it was there that as a boy of twelve, I first became interested in photography." So goes Alexander Alland's short narrative of his life as published in his book *American Counterpoint.* In 1923, just in his twenty-first year, he found himself pacing in the steerage of a boat within sight of Ellis Island, having fled civil war in Russia and a brief exile of three years in Istanbul. "How would I make myself understood, understand others?" he worried. The next evening he stood in Times Square, utterly fascinated by the people, the cars, the city lights. "For the first time in years I felt secure. Already I was one of the millions. I was an American."

For his first ten years in America, Alland (1902–1989) pieced together a living at numerous jobs, a few of which involved photography. Not until 1936 did his career as a photographer finally hit stride. He was commissioned to produce a photomural by the Federal Art Project for the Newark Public Library, and shortly thereafter he was asked to do the photographs for *Portrait of New York,* a book published at the time of the 1939 New York World's Fair. Alland's most important work was his book *American Counterpoint,* published in 1943, with essays by himself and Pearl Buck. Although there is often more variety and artistry in his photographs for *Portrait of New York, American Counterpoint* is the more focused vehicle for Alland's voice and vision. For Alland, being an American meant sharing "the desire for happiness, prosperity, and liberty," no matter what one's racial or national background might be. In his photography, he respected and celebrated those things that differentiated people, and at the same time, he tried to discern the ideals that seemed to unify people of many backgrounds. His own immigration experience gave him a strong respect for immigrants' conflicts between the desire to hold fast to the languages and traditions of the old country and the desire to learn the skills necessary to succeed in the new country. His photography ranged from images of great artistic elegance and force to journalistic images that strongly advocated his ideals of a democratic and multicultural society.

In the late forties Alland was blacklisted for his association with numerous "leftist" organizations, and he gave up making new photographs. Later in life he turned to photographic history and helped in the rediscovery of photographers such as Jacob Riis, Jesse Tarbox Beals, and Heinrich Tönnies. ◀

Self-Portrait, 1940s. Gelatin silver print, 24.7 by 19.7 cm. Courtesy Howard Greenberg Gallery, New York

Commandment Keepers Congregation, 1940. Gelatin silver print, 19.5 by 24.7 cm. Courtesy Howard Greenberg Gallery, New York

University of Chicago Students Prepare Placards for a Demonstration against Racial Discrimination in the Medical School, c. 1946. Gelatin silver print, 19.7 by 24.7 cm. Courtesy Howard Greenberg Gallery, New York

Turkish Americans, 1942. Gelatin silver print, 26.0 by 32.0 cm. Courtesy Howard Greenberg Gallery, New York

Facing page: *Photomontage,* c. 1943. Gelatin silver print, 30.5 by 25.5 cm. Courtesy Howard Greenberg Gallery, New York

Broad and Wall, c. 1939. Gelatin silver print, 23.9 by 16.7 cm.
Courtesy Howard Greenberg Gallery, New York

The Old Bridge, 1938. Gelatin silver print, 24.6 by 20.0 cm.
Courtesy Howard Greenberg Gallery, New York

Untitled, c. 1939. Gelatin silver print, 20.2 by 25.0 cm.
Courtesy Howard Greenberg Gallery, New York

Hooverville, 1938. Gelatin silver print, 19.8 by 25.3 cm.
Courtesy Howard Greenberg Gallery, New York

"WHEN OTTO AND I SET OUT that wintery Sunday, we went out together to find truth in life," Hansel Mieth wrote about the day she and Otto Hagel left Germany at the age of fifteen to wander throughout Europe, the Balkans, and Turkey. Mieth (born 1909) had suffered through poverty as her parents worked at demeaning jobs to make ends meet, and financial problems eventually forced her to leave the one place that she had hoped would turn her own life around—school.

Born into a working-class family in Germany, Otto Hagel (1909–1974) had already developed an interest in photography and music when he left school at the age of fourteen to be apprenticed to a Stuttgart watchmaker. Soon after, he met Hansel Mieth—whom he would eventually marry—and together they left their homes and country. This period of wandering and exploring seems to have been a crucial and exhilarating, if sometimes difficult, time for them. And things only seemed to get worse when they returned home to a hostile and suspicious welcome. Worried about the economic woes of Europe and the rise of fascism in Germany, Hagel emigrated to the United States in 1928 and soon made his way to San Francisco. Mieth followed in 1930. Together, they worked as laborers and migrant farm laborers, turning to free-lance photography and filmmaking whenever they could.

Through her friend and fellow photographer Peter Stackpole, Mieth eventually began to receive assignments from *Time* magazine. Unable to join the Works Progress Administration's Art Project because her photographs were determined to be too propagandistic, she joined it's Youth and Recreation Project instead, which led her to San Francisco's Mission District to photograph. Eventually, both Hagel and Mieth photographed for *Life*—Mieth became a staff photographer in 1937 and Hagel eventually worked for the magazine as a free-lance photographer—and they contributed a number of photographs and photographic essays over the years.

Always sympathetic with the side of labor and the unions, the two "wanted to bring about a better understanding of the reality of human existence . . . the contrast and chasm between rich and poor," as Mieth wrote. But ultimately, they began to realize that their status as reporters had slowly but surely turned them into bystanders where they had once been participants. Their hope that their photographs would change the minds of *Life* magazine's mass audience was little more than a sentimental, well-intentioned pipe dream.

In the 1940s, when magazine work became scarcer because of their political views, Hagel and Mieth acquired land north of San Francisco and began to take up chicken farming. The rewards, simple pleasures, hard work, and bad fortune that marked their attempt to live a self-sufficient, rural life are the subject of one of their most personal *Life* essays, "The Simple Life." ◄

Otto Hagel, *Tom Mooney,* 1938. Gelatin silver print, 34.3 by 26.5 cm. Collection Hansel Mieth

Otto Hagel, *The Widow, Tioga, North Dakota, Guadalcanal Casualty,* 1942. Gelatin silver print, 34.5 by 26.8 cm. Collection Hansel Mieth

Hansel Mieth, *Outstretched Hands*, 1934. Gelatin silver print, 26.4 by 34.4 cm. Center for Creative Photography

Otto Hagel, *Mississippi Orphan Band,* 1938. Gelatin
silver print, 26.6 by 34.2 cm. Center for Creative
Photography

Otto Hagel, *Eastside, New York,* 1938. Gelatin silver print, 33.5 by 25.6 cm. Collection Hansel Mieth

Otto Hagel, *Ford Workers at Union Hall,* 1940. Gelatin silver print, 34.5 by 26.5 cm. Collection Hansel Mieth

Otto Hagel, *German-American Bund,* 1938. Gelatin silver print, 26.5 by 34.5 cm. Collection Hansel Mieth

Hansel Mieth, *Flag Salute, Heart Mountain Internees,*
1942. Gelatin silver print, 26.2 by 34.5 cm. Collection
the artist

Hansel Mieth and Otto Hagel, *Sheriffs and Deputies,
1936 Lettuce Strike, Salinas,* 1936. Gelatin silver print,
23.5 by 33.9 cm. Collection Hansel Mieth

Facing page: **Hansel Mieth and Otto Hagel,** *Night
Meeting at the Cross Roads,* 1936. Gelatin silver print,
33.5 by 25.8 cm. Center for Creative Photography

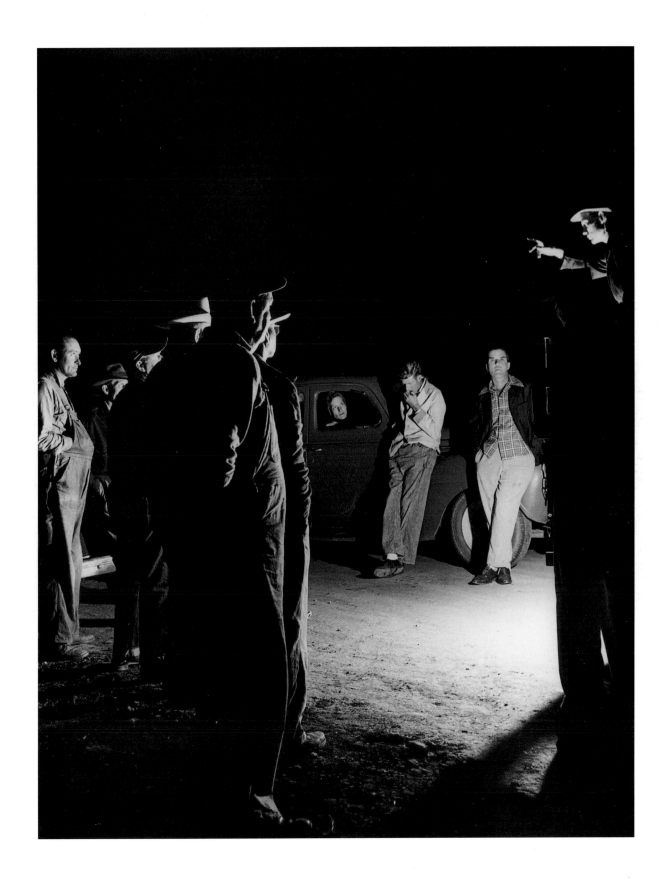

Hansel Mieth, *Rosie the Riveter, Mare Island Shipyard,* 1942.
Gelatin silver print, 34.5 by 26.6 cm. Collection the artist

Hansel Mieth, *The Weightmaster Is Waiting*, 1934. Gelatin
silver print, 34.3 by 26.4 cm. Collection the artist

Otto Hagel, Untitled, from *The Simple Life*, 1950.
Gelatin silver print, 34.3 by 26.0 cm. Collection
Hansel Mieth

Otto Hagel, Untitled, from *The Simple Life*, 1950.
Gelatin silver print, 34.3 by 26.0 cm. Collection
Hansel Mieth

Hansel Mieth and Otto Hagel, *End of the Road*, from
The Simple Life, 1950. Gelatin silver print, 26.5 by 34.3 cm.
Collection Hansel Mieth

Hansel Mieth and Otto Hagel, *Fence Pulling,*
from *The Simple Life,* 1950. Gelatin silver print,
26.4 by 34.1 cm. Center for Creative Photography

JOHN GUTMANN

"WHEN I CAME TO THIS COUNTRY I tried to find a job as a teacher which because of the Depression was impossible. . . . I really went to photography out of a need to try to make some money in this country. . . . And then I discovered right away that I was fascinated with this new way of seeing. It was a new medium! It was making its own rules for me."

Born in 1905, John Gutmann had trained and exhibited as a painter in Breslau and Berlin. In 1933, he decided that he could no longer stay in Germany, and he emigrated to the United States. Before leaving, though, he purchased a camera and arranged to sell photographs of America to German magazines and photography agencies.

For Gutmann, the simultaneity of emigrating and taking up photography was the ideal foundation for seeing and depicting an America in flux. The Germany that Gutmann had left behind had, arguably, the most experimental attitude toward photography in the world at that time. During the idealism of the Weimar period, German photographers tinkered with every aspect of the photographic process in their attempt to envision a new society and forge links with the revolutionary artists of the new Soviet Union. Gutmann's background as an artist—deeply embedded in Weimar culture and German expressionism—made him exceptionally receptive to segments of American culture overlooked by many American photographers.

Like many European photographers of the twenties and thirties, Gutmann cared little, if any, that the subject of his photography had little correspondence to the long history of Western art. Instead, he equated the camera with the human eye, which freed him to photograph whatever he saw and however he saw it. If he looked up in wonder at a multistory parking garage, his camera looked up, too. If he looked down onto a Nazi flag hanging in San Francisco's City Hall, his camera leaned over the railing with him and took in the entire scene.

In his first decade of American photography, Gutmann created an extraordinarily diverse and personal perspective on this nation. Photographing primarily in the street, he used his eye and camera to mirror America's commercial exuberance and its obsession with automobiles and guns. He captured the rhythm, flair, and tension of a multicultural, multiracial society that was unlike anything he had witnessed in his native Germany. He looked on with non-judgmental wonder as the eccentric, the flamboyant, and the outrageous passed right in front of his eyes. ◄

Self-Portrait with Lovebird, 1934. Gelatin silver print, 26.4
by 28.0 cm. Courtesy the artist and Fraenkel Gallery,
San Francisco

Declaration of Protest. Chinatown, San Francisco, 1935.
Gelatin silver print, 30.7 by 26.5 cm. Courtesy the artist
and Fraenkel Gallery, San Francisco

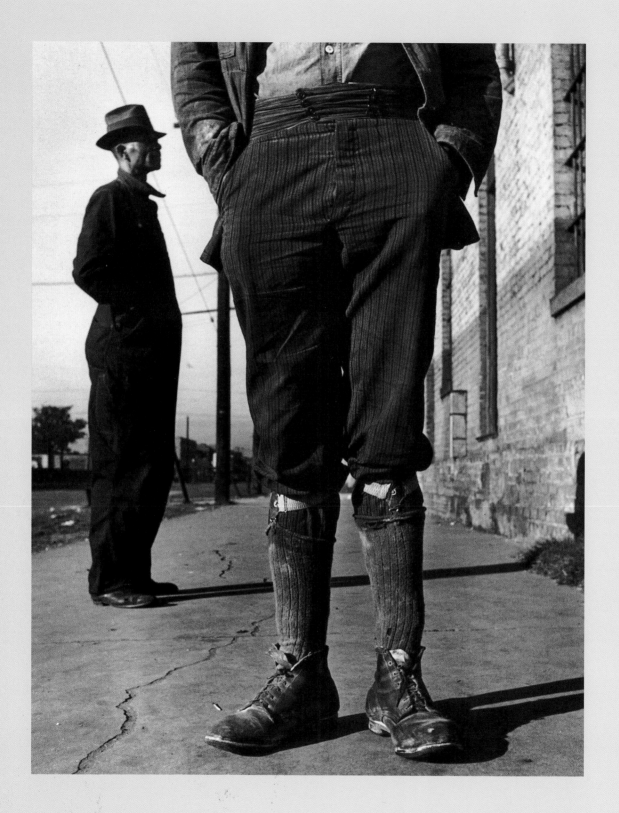

Mobile, Alabama, 1937. Gelatin silver print, 33.7 by 35.3 cm.
Courtesy the artist and Fraenkel Gallery, San Francisco

"WPA", San Francisco, 1937. Gelatin silver print, 33.2 by
25.7 cm. Courtesy the artist and Fraenkel Gallery, San
Francisco

Cynics. Hollywood, 1934. Gelatin silver print, 25.9 by 25.8 cm. Courtesy the artist and Fraenkel Gallery, San Francisco

Facing page: *Indian High School Band. Arizona*, 1937. Gelatin silver print, 33.6 by 19.3 cm. Courtesy the artist and Fraenkel Gallery, San Francisco

Portrait of Count Basie. San Francisco, 1939. Gelatin silver print, 31.5 by 35.7 cm. Courtesy the artist and Fraenkel Gallery, San Francisco

The Open Window. Philadelphia, 1939. Gelatin silver
print, 33.5 by 24.4 cm. Courtesy the artist and Fraenkel
Gallery, San Francisco

Dream of Uprising, 1935. Gelatin silver print, 18.3 by
24.0 cm. Center for Creative Photography

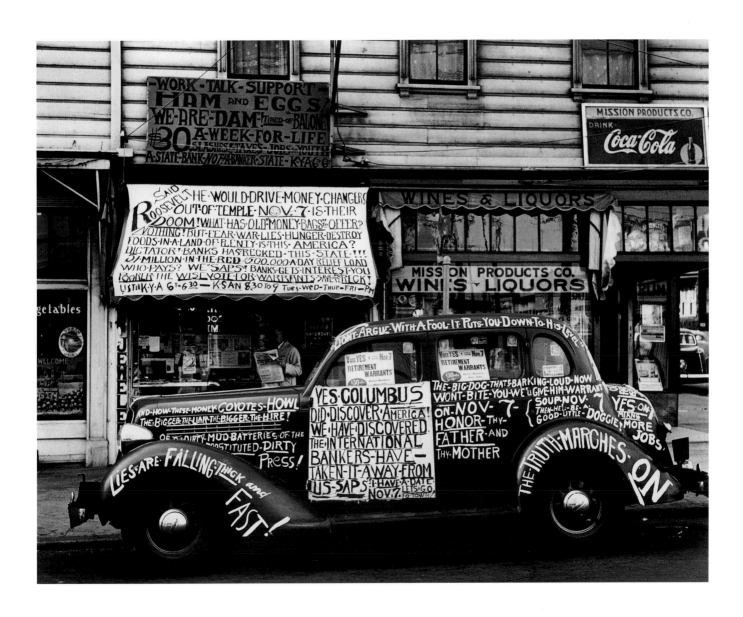

"Yes, Columbus Did Discover America!" San Francisco, 1938.
Gelatin silver print, 29.1 by 36.4 cm. Center for Creative
Photography

LISETTE MODEL

"I AM A PASSIONATE LOVER OF THE SNAPSHOT, because of all photographic images it comes closest to the truth," Lisette Model wrote in 1974. Although no one would ever mistake one of Model's own photographs for a snapshot, the strength of her photographs is derived from a powerful and unexpected directness and what almost appears to be a highly trained visual innocence.

Born Lisette Stern, in Vienna, to a Jewish, Austro-Czech father and an Italian mother, Lisette Model (1901–1983) originally studied piano and singing, with one of her teachers being composer Arnold Schönberg. In 1926 she moved with her family to France, where, in 1933, she suddenly and decisively switched from music to photography. One year later, in Nice, she began making a series of uncompromising and seemingly surreptitious pictures of gamblers and the leisure class as they sat "seeing and being seen" on the city's great and elite beachfront, the Promenade des Anglais.

In 1938, she and her husband Evsa Model, a Jewish, Russian-born painter, emigrated to New York City. Throughout the next decade, she photographed mainly on the streets of the city. Model, who left a Europe of aristocracy and privilege and whose brother was deported by Vichy France only to die in a concentration camp, seemed to be continually probing for the moral strengths and weaknesses of her new homeland. Although Model continually denied any overt social content in her photographs, it is easy to see that, as in Nice, her New York pictures pierced the expensive suits or worn woolens of whomever she encountered in search of the moral fiber that lay beneath. In her images, the rich seem disdainful of and largely disinterested in those who shine their shoes and those who sit defeated, exhausted, and ignored on their streets, while the poor and the working class manage a kind of defiant dignity and even occasionally enjoy themselves drinking, dancing, and making romance in small clubs off the Bowery.

Model's eye was often drawn toward a particular kind of inner strength exemplified by women—women who fell outside the mainstream American stereotype: overweight women in bathing suits at Coney Island or in clashing prints seated on park benches, stern immigrant women, and poor women whose only style consideration was what would keep them warm. At the same time, her photographs unmasked the American concept of glamour as depicted in the store windows of Fifth Avenue, or in the Hollywood movie poster she found dangling next to a scrawny, plucked chicken in the window of a Jewish delicatessen. ◄

World War II Rally, Lower East Side, c. 1943. Gelatin silver
print, 34.5 by 27.1 cm. Center for Creative Photography

Reflections, New York City, c. 1940. Gelatin silver print,
34.5 by 26.8 cm. Center for Creative Photography

Lower East Side, 1940. Gelatin silver print, 34.5 by 26.9 cm.
Center for Creative Photography

Petty Labor, New York City, 1940. Gelatin silver print,
34.3 by 27.1 cm. Center for Creative Photography

Facing page: Untitled, 1940s. Gelatin silver print,
34.4 by 27.0 cm. Center for Creative Photography

Window Reflections, Fifth Avenue, New York City, 1940. Gelatin silver print, 39.1 by 49.4 cm. Center for Creative Photography

Facing page: *Reflection, New York City,* 1940. Gelatin silver print, 34.5 by 26.8 cm. Center for Creative Photography

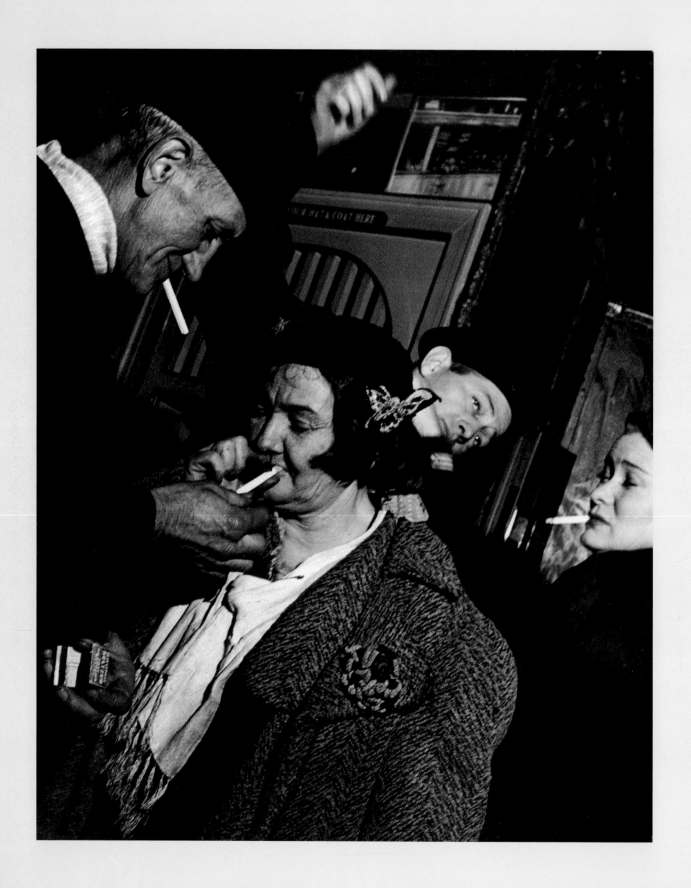

Singer at Sammy's, 1940. Gelatin silver print, 27.3 by 34.4
cm. Center for Creative Photography

Facing page: *Sammy's Bar,* 1940. Gelatin silver print, 34.5
by 27.6 cm. Center for Creative Photography

Coney Island, New York, 1942. Gelatin silver print, 26.7 by 34.3 cm. Center for Creative Photography

Fashion Show, Hotel Pierre, New York City, 1940. Gelatin
silver print, 39.1 by 48.8 cm. Center for Creative
Photography

MARION PALFI

"**I** CAME TO THE UNITED STATES IN 1940 at a very tragic time in human history and (it might sound corny) there was this man Roosevelt President and he talked to the people on the radio and told about the Four Freedoms and the better world of tomorrow. One day I told myself, perhaps I can help with my camera, " Marion Palfi recalled. Born in Berlin of Hungarian and German parents, Palfi (1907–1978) followed her father's career onto the German stage and into films. In 1932, she abandoned this direction and apprenticed herself to a Berlin portrait photographer, and she was soon photographing for German magazines. In 1936, worried about the situation in Germany, she moved to Amsterdam and opened up a portrait studio there, only to flee the German army four years later.

Once settled in New York City, America's racial intolerance and its growing urban problems shocked Palfi. Working in a photo-finishing lab to support herself, she began to develop an idea to counteract what she saw—a photographic project celebrating America's minority artists. This would be the first of nearly a dozen, large photographic essays that would consume her for the next three decades. Exhibited in 1945, *Great American Artists of Minority Groups* opened doors for her, including a Rosenwald fellowship the following year. As a result of meeting Black writers Langston Hughes (who continued to be her supporter until his death) and Arna Bontemps, Palfi was asked to photograph for a number of African American causes, and had one of her photographs appear on the cover of the first issue of *Ebony.*

After the success of this first project, never again would Palfi photograph simply for her own pleasure. She began to describe herself as a "social research photographer" or as a combination "sociologist, anthropologist, psychologist." Each of her photographs became a compact narrative that, as part of a larger project, represented an exploration into the societies that remain "invisible in America," to quote the title of a book devoted to her work. Full of passion, Palfi's images clearly indicate where her sympathies lie.

In the next ten years, this small woman with a German accent and a camera slung around her neck photographed in nearly every type of environment, from the lynching towns of the South to the worst urban slums in America. She worked on projects dealing with major social problems: for example, the book, *Suffer Little Children,* on poverty and children; two series, *Georgia Study* and *There Is No More Time,* on racial discrimination in the South; and the series, *In These Ten Cities,* on housing discrimination. As she put it, the end of discrimination will not only free the oppressed, "it will free US—will make US whole human beings." ◄

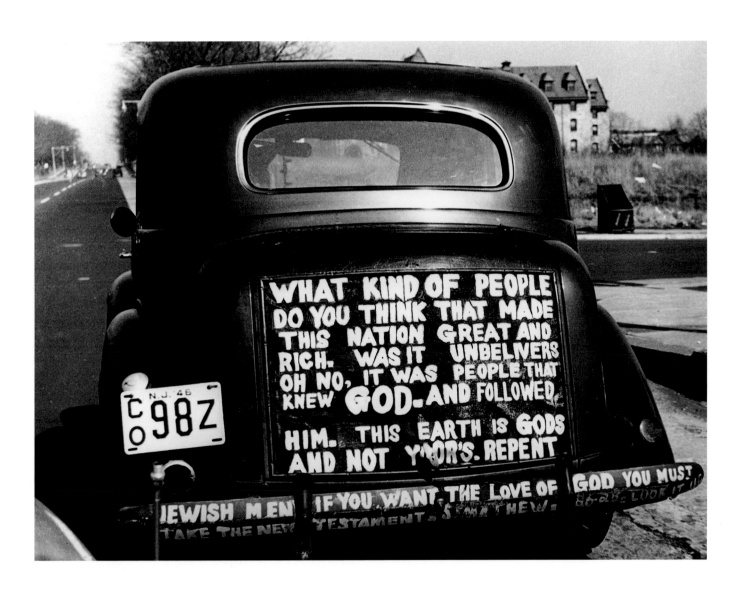

New Jersey Car, from *Signs of Discrimination,* 1946–49.
Gelatin silver print, 26.4 by 34.5 cm. Center for Creative
Photography

Somewhere in the South, 1946–49. Gelatin silver print,
24.2 by 19.0 cm. Center for Creative Photography

Dean Dixon after One of His "Concerts for Young People,"
from *Great American Artists of Minority Groups*, 1944–45.
Gelatin silver print, 42.6 by 35.1 cm. Center for Creative
Photography

Jehovah's Witness about 12 Years Old, Lakeview, Florida, from
Children in America, 1947. Gelatin silver print, 34.3 by
26.4 cm. Center for Creative Photography

The Columbians in Atlanta, the "Juvenile Delinquents of the
Ku Klux Klan," from *Suffer Little Children*, 1946–49.
Gelatin silver print, 34.1 by 26.3 cm. Center for Creative
Photography

Los Angeles, Anti Klan Meeting Where Klan Did Strike, from *Signs of Discrimination*, 1946–49. Gelatin silver print, 34.6 by 42.2 cm. Center for Creative Photography

Facing page: *Washington D.C., In the Shadow of the Capitol*, from *Suffer Little Children*, 1946–49. Gelatin silver print, 34.8 by 26.6 cm. Center for Creative Photography

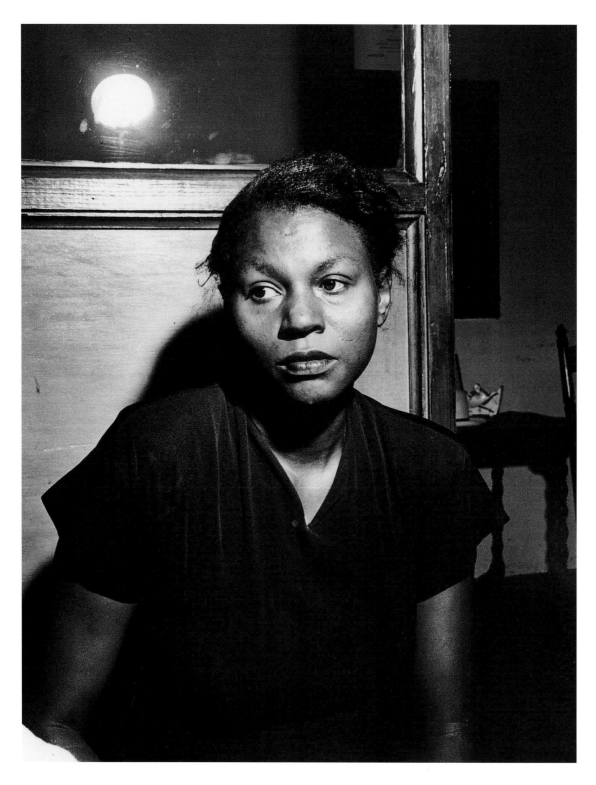

Wife of a Lynch Victim, Irwinton, Georgia, from *There Is No More Time,* 1949. Gelatin silver print, 34.4 by 26.9 cm. Center for Creative Photography

Atlanta, from *Georgia Study*, 1949. Gelatin silver print, 35.0 by 27.1 cm. Center for Creative Photography

ROBERT FRANK

"WHEN I GOT TO AMERICA I saw right away that everything was open, that you could do anything. And how you were accepted just depended on what you did with it. You could work to satisfy what was in you. Once I came to America I knew I wouldn't go back." At the end of World War One, Robert Frank's father emigrated from Germany to Switzerland, married, and set up an importing business. Born in Zurich in 1924, Frank was fifteen when war broke out again in Europe. Later, he said that "being Jewish and living with the threat of Hitler must have been a very big part of my understanding of people that were put down or who were held back."

During the war years, Frank decided to take up photography as a way of escaping the restrictions of his family and, eventually, of Switzerland. Between 1949 and 1953, Frank visited New York City frequently and traveled extensively throughout Europe and South America, finding his style and earning a living by commissions for magazines like *Harper's Bazaar* and *McCall's*. The more he worked for magazines, the more he became embittered and disillusioned at the concessions they repeatedly demanded of him. Full of self-confidence and passion, Frank applied for, and received, a John Simon Guggenheim Memorial Fellowship in 1955. He, his artist wife Mary, and their two children set off in their car on a series of cross-country expeditions during 1955 and 1956.

The result, nearly five years later, was a book of Frank's photographs called *The Americans*, which is now widely regarded as a high-water mark in twentieth century American photography. In photographs that are at once bleak and tender, Frank captured the breadth of the American continent, the despair, hypocrisy, and loneliness that seemed to pervade American society, and the emptiness that lay behind the facade of Hollywood and consumer hype that masqueraded as the good life.

But Frank's style and the photographs he made for *The Americans* were not always received well at first. When *U.S. Camera* published a number of these photographs in 1958, the editor felt compelled to note that "Robert Frank's vision of America certainly isn't everyone's picture of the country we live in. This is hardly the inspirational school of photography."

Aware that his photographs were being viewed as a harsh criticism of his adopted country, Frank responded: "Life for a photographer cannot be a matter of indifference. Opinion often consists of a kind of criticism. But criticism can come out of love. It is important to see what is invisible to others. Perhaps the look of hope or the look of sadness." Frank made the invisible visible by abusing, as it were, what the previous generation of photographers had seen as the basic tools of photography. He frequently used the angle and point of view of his camera to comment on his subject, to capture the precise moment when a small gesture or visual relationship could undermine the meaning of the central element in the picture. Through selective focus or insufficient lighting he could render entire sections of the photograph deliberately illegible to suit his expressive needs. He compressed space to heighten the sense of congestion and to force comparisons between disparate visual elements.

What Frank seemed to have intuitively recognized was how to render visually, in a manner that was both profound and poetic, the widening dysfunctionality between the public-relations image of America and the reality as experienced by ordinary people day in and day out. As Jack Kerouac put it, writing in the introduction to the U.S. edition of *The Americans:* "Robert Frank, Swiss, unobtrusive, nice, with that little camera that he raises and snaps with one hand he sucked a sad poem right out of America onto film, taking rank among the tragic poets of the world." ◄

En Route from New York to Washington, Club Car, 1955–56.
Gelatin silver print, 21.6 by 33.0 cm. Courtesy The
Museum of Fine Arts, Houston; The Target Collection
of American Photography: Museum purchase with
funds provided by the Target Stores

Bar, Detroit, 1955–56. Gelatin silver print, 31.7 by 47.6 cm.
Courtesy Philadelphia Museum of Art: Purchased with
funds given by Dorothy Norman

Movie Premiere, Hollywood, 1955–56. Gelatin silver print, 31.6 by 21.3 cm. Center for Creative Photography

Political Rally, Chicago, 1956. Gelatin silver print, 50.8 by 40.3 cm. Courtesy Philadelphia Museum of Art: Purchased with funds given by Dorothy Norman

Convention Hall, Chicago, 1955–56. Gelatin silver print,
21.3 by 31.7 cm. Courtesy The Museum of Fine Arts,
Houston: Museum purchase with funds provided by Charter
Bancshares, Inc. and Jerry E. Finger, Chairman, Charter
Bancshares, Inc.

Facing page: *Contact Sheet #18*, 1956. Gelatin silver developed-
out print, proof sheet, 25.3 by 20.3 cm. Courtesy Robert
Frank Collection, Gift of Robert Frank, © 1995 Board of
Trustees, National Gallery of Art, Washington, D.C.

SELECTED BIBLIOGRAPHY

ALEXANDER ALLAND
Alland, Alexander. *American Counterpoint.* New York: John Day Co., 1943.

Riesenberg, Felix and Alexander Alland. *Portrait of New York.* New York: Macmillan, 1939.

Yochelson, Bonnie. *The Committed Eye: Alexander Alland's Photography.* New York: Museum of the City of New York, 1991.

ROBERT FRANK
Alexander, Stuart. *Robert Frank: A Bibliography, Filmography, and Exhibition Chronology, 1946–1985.* Tucson, Ariz.: Center for Creative Photography, 1986.

Frank, Robert. *The Americans.* New York: Grove Press, 1959.

Frank, Robert. *The Lines of My Hand.* New York: Pantheon, 1989.

Greenough, Sarah and Philip Brookman. *Robert Frank: Moving Out.* Washington, D.C.: National Gallery of Art, 1994.

Tucker, Anne Wilkes. *Robert Frank: New York to Nova Scotia.* Boston, Mass.: Little, Brown, 1986.

JOHN GUTMANN
Gutmann, John. *As I Saw It: Photographs.* San Francisco, Calif.: San Francisco Museum of Modern Art, 1976.

Phillips, Sandra S. *John Gutmann: Beyond the Document.* San Francisco, Calif.: San Francisco Museum of Modern Art, 1989.

Sutnik, Maia-Mari. *Gutmann, August 24–October 20, 1985.* Toronto: Art Gallery of Ontario, 1985.

Thomas, Lew, ed. *The Restless Decade: John Gutmann's Photographs of the Thirties.* New York: H. N. Abrams, 1984.

OTTO HAGEL
Goldblatt, Louis and Otto Hagel. *Men and Machines.* San Francisco, Calif.: International Longshoreman's and Warehouseman's Union, 1963

HANSEL MIETH AND OTTO HAGEL
Mieth, Hansel and Otto Hagel. *The Simple Life: Photographs from America, 1929–1971.* Stuttgart, Ger.: Schmetterling, 1991.

LISETTE MODEL
Model, Lisette. *Lisette Model. The Archive* 4. Tucson, Ariz.: Center for Creative Photography, 1977.

Model, Lisette. *Lisette Model.* Millerton, N.Y.: Aperture, 1979.

Thomas, Ann. *Lisette Model.* Ottawa, Ont.: National Gallery of Canada, 1990.

MARION PALFI
Coleman, A. D. "Marion Palfi: My Studio Is the World." *Camera & Darkroom* 15, no. 10 (October 1993): pp. 42–51.

Enyeart, James L. *Invisible in America: an Exhibition of Photographs by Marion Palfi.* Lawrence, Kan.: University of Kansas Museum of Art, 1973.

Lindquist-Cock, Elizabeth. *Marion Palfi. The Archive* 19. Tucson, Ariz.: Center for Creative Photography, 1983.

Sorgenfrei, Robert and David Peters, comp. *Marion Palfi Archive. Guide Series* 10. Tucson, Ariz.: Center for Creative Photography, 1985.

The University of Arizona's Center for Creative Photography is a museum devoted to the history of photography as an art form since 1900. The Center houses the complete photographic archives of more than thirty photographers who helped shape the art of photography during the twentieth century. A surprising number of those photographers were first- or second-generation immigrants from Europe, reflecting the social and political traumas that affected that continent for much of the first half of the century. Their European upbringing and artistic training contributed greatly to the radical transformation of American photography, culminating in what must be considered a highwater mark in American photography—the publication of Robert Frank's 1955 and 1956 photographs in *The Americans.*

I am indebted to many people for their assistance in research, providing slides and reproduction prints, and in securing invaluable loans and permissions: Peter MacGill and Pace/MacGill Gallery, New York; Howard Greenberg, Howard Greenberg Gallery, New York; Jeffery Fraenkel and Fraenkel Gallery, San Francisco; Debra Heimerdinger, Vision Gallery, San Francisco; Hansel Mieth; John Gutmann; Alexander Alland, Jr. and Sonia Alland; Martin Magner; Peter C. Marzio, Director, and Anne Tucker, Gus Lyndall Wortham Curator of Photography, The Museum of Fine Arts, Houston; Martha Chahroudi, Philadelphia Museum of Art; Ann Thomas, National Gallery of Canada; Sarah Greenough, National Gallery of Art, Washington, D.C.; John G. Morris; Teresa Engle. Finally, I want to thank Andrei Codrescu—poet, writer, and commentator on all things American—for his insightful essay.

All of the staff of the Center for Creative Photography have participated in making this exhibition and book possible, but I would like to especially credit the efforts of Sharon Alexandra, Leslie Calmes, Dianne Nilsen, Cass Fey, Shelly Jurmain, Dustin Leavitt, Nancy Lutz, Margie Puerta, Amy Rule, Keith Schreiber, Nancy Solomon, Anne Sullivan, and Marcia Tiede. Betsi Meissner, the Center's 1994/95 Ansel Adams Intern, dedicated herself to many aspects of this project and made many helpful contributions.

Terence Pitts, Director
Center for Creative Photography
University of Arizona

Marion Palfi, *Saturday, Louisville, Georgia,* 1949. Gelatin silver print, 34.8 by 26.9 cm. Center for Creative Photography